BECOMING W

My Soul's Journey

A GUIDED JOURNAL BY CAROL KENT & KAREN LEE-THORP

The Navigators is an international Christian organization. Our mission is to reach, disciple, and equip people to know Christ and to make Him known through successive generations. We envision multitudes of diverse people in the United States and every other nation who have a passionate love for Christ, live a lifestyle of sharing Christ's love, and multiply spiritual laborers among those without Christ.

NavPress is the publishing ministry of The Navigators. NavPress publications help believers learn biblical truth and apply what they learn to their lives and ministries. Our mission is to stimulate spiritual formation among our readers.

© 2002 by Speak Up, Inc.
All rights reserved. No part of this publication may be reproduced in any form without written permission from NavPress, P.O. Box 35001, Colorado Springs, CO 80935. www.navpress.com

Library of Congress Catalog Card Number: 2001044759
ISBN 1-57683-300-3

Cover design by Dan Jamison
Cover and interior illustrations by Kristina Swarner
Creative Team: Nanci McAlister, Lori Mitchell, Glynese Northam

Excerpts taken from *Tame Your Fears*, *Secret Longings of the Heart*, and *Becoming a Woman of Influence*.

Unless otherwise identified, all Scripture quotations in this publication are taken from the *HOLY BIBLE: NEW INTERNATIONAL VERSION®* (NIV®). Copyright © 1973, 1978, 1984 by International Bible Society. Used by permission of Zondervan Publishing House. All rights reserved. Other versions used include: *The Message: New Testament with Psalms and Proverbs* by Eugene H. Peterson, copyright © 1993, 1994, 1995, used by permission of NavPress Publishing Group; the *New Revised Standard Version* (NRSV), copyright © 1989, by the Division of Christian Education of the National Council of the Churches of Christ in the USA, used by permission, all rights reserved.

Kent, Carol, 1947-
    Becoming who God wants me to be : a guided journal / Carol Kent and Karen Lee-Thorp.
        p. cm.
    ISBN 1-56783-300-3
    1. Christian women--Religious life. I. Lee-Thorp, Karen. II. title.
BV4527 .K449 2002
248.8'43--dc21   2001044759

Printed in the United States of America
1 2 3 4 5 6 7 8 9 10 / 05 04 03 02

FOR A FREE CATALOG OF
NAVPRESS BOOKS & BIBLE STUDIES,
CALL 1-800-366-7788 (USA)
OR 1-416-499-4615 (CANADA)

Contents

HOW TO USE *My Soul's Journey*

God made you. God formed you to play an essential role in the story He has been writing ever since He first had the idea to make the universe. Maybe you wonder whether your role could be very important. But it is.

God chose your DNA and your family, knowing that as good or as mixed-up as they were, they would launch you into becoming the you He wanted. God has led you through experiences that have shaped you—and that you have shaped. None of it has been wasted; all of it has equipped you to be who you were meant to be.

My Soul's Journey will help you think through your past and present with an eye to your future. You'll unearth your deepest longings and free them from any negative patterns that may have grown up around them. You'll find a path out of the maze of fear into the wide-open spaces of courage. And you'll discover how your life experiences, even the darkest ones, have equipped you to be a valuable gift to the people around you.

My Soul's Journey flows from inward searching to outward giving. But it's your journal—you can use it however you find most helpful. Feel free to start with whatever exercises get at what's on your mind. You can write in the journal, draw, cut out pictures from magazines and paste them in, use an exercise as a springboard to prayer, or just read a section and think about it.

If you want to explore your early life, turn to "History of Me." If you're mad, look at "Rage." If you're sad, check out "Sorrow." If you want to figure out what you have to offer others, look at "My Gifts."

Each of the main sections ("History of Me," "My Longings," "My Fears," and "My Gifts") traces a process by which you can move from feeling stuck in a negative pattern to being free to choose a positive one. You may want to work through all the stages of one of those processes, or you may decide to skip the stages that don't seem relevant to you.

Even if you don't consider yourself an artist, you might want to play with doodling or pasting pictures in your journal. Sometimes images say more to your heart than words. And don't worry if you don't have clear words for what you want to say. Nobody will be grading your essays. Sometimes a simple list or jumble of words will say it all.

Enjoy yourself. In God's arms, you're a kid. This is a place to say whatever lies deep in your heart. Whatever you write, God will gather it up into His own heart, full of tenderness and joy to see you spreading your wings.

Dear Friend,

As I look in the rearview mirror of my life, I see lots of inward, heart issues I needed to deal with before I could be effective in my outward journey of ministering to others. Maybe you've found this to be true in your life.

Having come to know Christ as a child, I wanted to live for something that would last forever. But unfulfilled expectations, fears, and a sense of powerlessness hindered me from pursuing God's call on my life. For a while (like many women), I believed I was unattractive, moderately intelligent, and organizationally challenged. I wondered what God could do with my life that would be important for His kingdom and valuable to others. I wanted to know who I was in His eyes, but when I looked into the mirror, I felt inadequate and "not quite special enough" to do something great for God. I struggled with longings for significance, security, intimacy, success, and spirituality. The Enemy plagued me with a series of lies:

> ❧ I'm not worth anything.
> ❧ If I'm a good person, God will protect me from pain and suffering.
> ❧ If I'm a good Christian, I won't have relationship struggles.
> ❧ A woman who trusts God doesn't experience anger, depression, or hopelessness.

Trudging through this inward jungle, I faced fearful situations and crucial choices. A mandatory speech class in college paralyzed me with the fear of making a fool of myself in front of my peers. But as I forced myself to risk embarrassment, I discovered a new freedom. I started to enjoy preparing the speeches and motivating the listeners to action. Each time I forced myself to face fear instead of retreating, I gained important momentum for the next situation.

The most important step in my journey of the soul was realizing that I fed my emotional responses to disappointments and fearful situations through the grid of my belief system. I started to see that my actions were direct responses to what I believed about God and His Word. If my belief system was grounded in Truth, my passions and actions were honorable and holy. However, if I believed the Enemy's lies, my choices frustrated me and sometimes harmed others.

Whether choosing a career, selecting a college major, accepting a marriage proposal, or facing a personal crisis, I needed to learn the Bible's principles to deal with the choices I would face for the rest of my life. Whenever I stepped into uncharted territory, I faced fear. Sometimes it was mild anxiety, and sometimes it was a powerful paralysis that kept me bound up in a self-made prison.

Then something new happened. I realized that every time I faced my fear, admitting the sorrow of feeling helpless and letting the brokenness free me to admit I couldn't help myself, I was brought to a place of surrender and was able to make faith-filled decisions. It didn't happen all at once. It was a process, an inward journey that took me from expectations, through disappointments and a wide range of emotions, to decisions based on God's Word.

As I moved through the fear, I gained a new sense of security in God's ability to take a girl with low self-esteem and transform her into a woman of faith, confidence, and action. My life was forever changed. Slowly at first, then more often, I realized that other women were coming to me for advice, biblical counsel, prayer, and encouragement. In the early years I was afraid to speak of my failures and my inward search for meaning, but I soon realized the women who were asking questions identified much more personally with my failures than they did with my successes. God wasn't asking me to be perfect. He was asking me to be real and to simply share my journey, including the unfulfilled expectations and disappointments. It wasn't a matter of having lived perfectly. All He required was honesty, vulnerability, and a willingness to point women to His Truth.

The purpose of this journal is to guide you through your own inward path of discovering who you are in Christ. Once you have discovered your intrinsic worth to Him, you'll be able to face your fears and turn them into faith as you find yourself becoming a woman of influence who is pointing others to Jesus. The first three sections—History of Me, My Longings, and My Fears—will lead you on an inward journey. The last section—My Gifts—will aid you in your outward journey. This journal draws its inspiration from three of my books: *Secret Longings of the Heart, Tame Your Fears,* and *Becoming a Woman of Influence.*

Enjoy the ride! Document your feelings. Be honest. Be observant. Talk out loud with someone else when you discover something new. Don't quit when you come to a hard question. Pause and ask God to reveal your motives, your passions, and your purpose. Then respond. You'll discover the greatest joy is using what you've learned to help someone else. There's no going back. This experience will forever change your life. You will become a woman of influence!

Wishing you Joy in the Journey,

Carol Kent

History of Me

Taking stock of your memories is like searching the refrigerator when you're hungry: What ingredients are in there that can be cooked into a decent meal? Maybe you think your fridge is bare. Maybe you cringe at the idea of opening the vegetable drawer for fear of the mold that may be lurking there. But God can feed thousands of people on scraps, so He knows there's plenty in your fridge. Mold doesn't bother Him. So take hold of God's hand, and with Him to steady you, open the door of your past.

God, when I think about looking back at my life, I just want to say

If you have trouble remembering things as they were, try whatever will help you remember:
Look through old photographs.
Play a song you loved back then.
Ask family members.
Read old letters.
Close your eyes and picture your bedroom when you were ten years old.
Ask God to bring back what He thinks is important.

INFLUENCES

Make a list of people, events, and experiences that have helped to shape who you have become. Events are mostly things that happened on a particular day or over a few days, like the day your brother or sister was born. Experiences are things that went on for a while, like Sunday school each week.

People

Events

Experiences

Strengths I've acquired during my journey

I'm Nobody! Who are you?
Are you — Nobody — too?
Then there's a pair of us! Don't tell!
They'd advertise — you know.
— Emily Dickinson

MEMORIES OF GOD

My earliest awareness of God was

When I was ten I thought God was

At fourteen I thought God was

My family thought God was

I believed in

I knew people who believed

12

What kept me away from God

What drew me to God

Some places I looked for God

Things I didn't understand about God were

I knew I was on the right track when

Memories of God

What I believe about God today

What got me here

God diligently trails after us without hurrying us. He speaks to us, letting us know that apart from Him we will never be complete.
—Jan Johnson

What I'm grateful for

Things I still wonder about

Our God specializes in working
through normal people who believe
in a supernormal God who will do
His work through them.
—Bruce Wilkinson

FAMILY TREE

Maybe your family grew straight up to the sky like a cedar. Maybe your family tree was more like a tangled shrub, knotted up by harsh winds. What were some of the qualities of your family members?

Grandparents:

Mom's mom   Mom's dad   Dad's mom   Dad's dad

Stepgrandparents
and assorted relatives

Parents:

Mom   Dad   Stepparents and others

Me

Siblings
(and half-siblings, stepsiblings, cousins, and the rest)

Qualities I admire in my family

Family qualities I want to lose

One thing I longed for from my family growing up

One fear I had growing up

I wanted to become

God never wastes our pain.

18

HEROES

One person I admire is

because

Qualities I admire

Qualities that really annoy me

What does this say about me?

My Longings

All of us experience emotional stress and spiritual conflict because of two basic facts about humans:

Women (and men) are created in the image of God. Because of God's image, natural man (woman) has tremendous potential—intellectually, artistically, and socially. She has a mind and body fashioned after her Maker's. She has an inborn, natural inclination to live as she was created to live—for God's glory, using her individual creativity to make the world a better place and to develop meaningful relationships with other people. But. . .

Women (and men) also have a sinful nature at war with their spiritual nature, even after they have accepted Christ as their Savior. Eve, the first woman, rebelled against God, and her daughters all inherit that rebellious nature. Our sinful nature tends to pervert and distort our purpose. Our sin and others' sin frustrates our highest calling to live like Christ, totally free and at one with the Father.

The tension between these two facts sets in motion a painful process. First, our natural potential to create and relate leads us to expect certain things from life. But our own and others' sin frustrates those expectations. Our unfulfilled expectations lead to disappointment, which in turn causes us to long for change or restoration. Our longings spark emotions. Our belief system determines how we decide to respond to those emotions. Those decisions set both the ruling passion of our lives and the actions that grow out of that ruling passion. The pattern looks like what you see on page 22.

In this section of *My Soul's Journey*, you'll explore how this process is working in your life. When you're conscious of your expectations, disappointments, longings, emotions, and beliefs, you'll have greater freedom to adjust your beliefs and thereby make better decisions, live by more fruitful passions, and take the best possible actions.

LONGINGS: A CHAIN REACTION

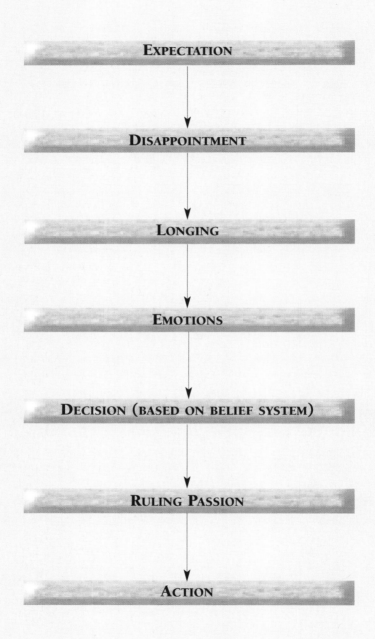

EXPECTATION

↓

DISAPPOINTMENT

↓

LONGING

↓

EMOTIONS

↓

DECISION (BASED ON BELIEF SYSTEM)

↓

RULING PASSION

↓

ACTION

EXPECTATIONS

In a way, our expectations about life are perfectly reasonable. They are based on what our lives *should* be and *would* be like if humankind had never sinned. They grow from our nature as bearers of God's image. Our expectations are doomed to disappointment because our world is far from that perfection, but that doesn't make our expectations "wrong." They are natural results of the way God designed us.

What expectations about life are hiding in your heart? Mark each of the following expectations that you've had:

☐ To be loved and affirmed by my parents

☐ To have parents who loved and affirmed each other

☐ To be healthy throughout my life into old age

☐ To meet a great guy who loves me and is committed to me

☐ To get into a good school

☐ To have a particular man stick by me

☐ To have a happy Christian marriage in which both partners seek God-honoring goals

☐ To have satisfying sexual and emotional intimacy with my husband

☐ To raise lovely, healthy children in a positive environment

☐ To send my grown children out to be productive members of society

☐ To see my children marry and have happy, healthy families

☐ To do meaningful work that contributes to the world's good and expresses my abilities

☐ To be valued in my work

☐ To provide essential food, shelter, and other needs for myself (and/or children, and/or aging parents)

☐ To own a home

☐ To be respected by coworkers and neighbors

☐ To have intimate relationships with faithful friends

☐ To be deeply understood by at least a few people

☐ To live in a stable neighborhood over a long period of time

☐ To have a sense of deep belonging to a church

☐ To have partners in fulfilling my calling in life

☐ To have a relatively stress-free life as long as I remain faithful to the Lord

☐ To have a constant awareness of God's closeness

☐ To feel successful

Other expectations

Of the ones you marked, put a star by each expectation that is being satis-fied in your life.

Put an X beside each expectation that has not been satisfied.

On a scale of 1 to 10, how content are you in various aspects of your life? What would it take to get to 10?

family

friends

love life

career

creativity

finances

body

emotions

intellect

Expectations

faith

26

When I think about my expectations, I feel

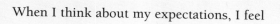

I wish

The confusing thing about expectations is

DISAPPOINTMENTS

Some disappointments are like knife wounds to the heart. Others are dull, throbbing aches.

- Your parent was cruel.
- Your child died.
- Your marriage never happened.
- You don't seem to have any really close friends where you live now.
- Your spouse or best friend betrayed you.
- Your child disappointed you.
- God seems a million miles away.

Of all my disappointed expectations, the ones that hurt the most are

because

Hope deferred makes the heart sick,
but a longing fulfilled is a tree of life.
Proverbs 13:12

What does your disappointment look like? Is it a face? Does it have a body or just a shape? What color is it? Draw your disappointment, or cut a picture out of a magazine that represents your disappointment. Or, if you like words better than pictures, describe your disappointment.

True atheists do not, I presume, feel disappointed in God. They expect nothing and receive nothing. But those who commit their lives to God, no matter what, instinctively expect something in return. Are those expectations wrong?
—Philip Yancey

Thinking about my disappointment makes me want to

You may have developed some ways of numbing the pain of your disappointments. Some of those ways may not be good for you or for others. Maybe you eat a lot and then throw up. Maybe you work too much or shut out your family with a wall of television. You probably know that numbing the pain isn't doing you or others any good. Instead, you need (1) to acknowledge the pain in the light of God's healing presence, and (2) find healthful, God-honoring ways of soothing yourself while you uncover the pain layer by layer.

What is one good thing you can do for yourself that does no harm either to you or to anyone else? You could:

&. Take a hot bath
&. Call a friend
&. Rent a really funny movie
&. Get a massage
&. Take a long walk
&. Listen to music
&. Read a book on a topic that sparks your passion
&. Eat (a little!) chocolate

Things I can do for myself when I'm by myself

Things I can do for myself that involve other people

What I'd like to say to God about my disappointment

LONGINGS

It's hard to sit still with disappointment. We move naturally to a longing for change—from disappointment to satisfaction, from loss to restoration. Longings come in all shapes and sizes, but there are some common categories:

THE LONGING TO MATTER

> I want to feel special.
> > I want to do something worthwhile.

THE LONGING TO POSSESS

> I want a baby.
> > I want a husband.
> > > I want a healthy body.
> > > > I want a beautiful body.
> > > > > I want a better job.

THE LONGING TO ESCAPE

> I want out of this marriage.
> > I want this rat race of busyness to end.
> > > I want to be free from anger.
> > > > I want to go home to God in heaven.

THE LONGING TO TRANSFORM

> I want to move from envy to contentment.
> > I want a more positive outlook on life.

THE LONGING TO TRANSCEND

> I want to change the law to make it more just.
> > I want to bring the message of Christ to the people in my town.

I want

I want

I want

I need

I need

I need

I really really really really long for

I don't think I long for anything.

Why is that?

It's scary to long for things because

Longings

What does God think about my longings?

It's hard for me to admit what I really long for.

I wish I longed for

I feel confused about my longings because

What I'd like to say to God about my longings is

*When we seek [God] with all
the longing He has planted in
our hearts, in the end, we
simply discover Him seeking
us, loving us — in all times
and all places.
—Sue Monk Kidd*

36

EMOTIONS

Longings spark intense emotions:

> 🐾 anger (fury, rage)
>> 🐾 sadness (depression, grief, despair)
>>> 🐾 fear (anxiety, terror, doubt)
>>>> 🐾 shame (humiliation, guilt)
> 🐾 joy (excitement, anticipation)
>> 🐾 strength (confidence, courage, determination)

When I think about my longings, I feel

because

I believe in the sun even when it is not shining. I believe in love even when feeling it not. I believe in God even when He is silent.
—Inscription on a cellar wall in Cologne, Germany, where Jews hid from Nazis

37

Draw or describe a picture of your emotions. Do they look like a huge gaping mouth? An explosion? A puddle? Fireworks and balloons? A dark closet?

I don't feel anything. I feel numb. Or dead. I think that underneath my numbness is

Turn back to page 31. You wrote some ideas for good things you could do for your-self to handle disappointment. What other ideas can you add? What can you do for yourself today to handle your emotions without going numb? It's helpful to come up with a variety of options so you'll have something you can do to nurture your-self whether it's daytime or nighttime, sunny or rainy, alone or with others.

Thinking about my feelings makes me want to

Instead, I'll

What does God think about my feelings?

If you want to explore your emotions more deeply now, turn to the second section of this journal ("My Fears") and use the questions on powerlessness, rage/anger/depression, denial, sorrow, etc.

BELIEFS

We don't just sit around having longings and feelings. We decide to do something. Or we decide to *avoid* doing something. These decisions aren't random—they're based on our deepest beliefs and assumptions about life. We may not be consciously aware of those beliefs, but we can track them down by looking at what we decided to do. Some typical beliefs (some are realistic; others are not) are:

- If I'm a good Christian, life should be fair.
- It's a sin to feel depressed (or angry, or afraid).
- If God loved me, bad things wouldn't happen to me.
- It's silly to feel so much grief about my little problem when there's so much real tragedy in the world.
- My value in the world is determined by _____.
- I don't have a husband (or a *good* husband, or a close friend) because I'm not lovable.
- If I don't have _____, then I'll die.
- If I'm rejected (or if I fail), then I'll die.
- I can't trust anybody.
- No matter what happens, I'm securely loved by a God who is committed to my good.
- God wants to give me love and support through other people.
- There are people in the world whom I can depend on.
- My suffering grieves God.
- I can take advantage of suffering to pursue growth.
- Failure is never final.
- Failure offers a chance for learning.
- I'm designed to make a unique and valuable contribution to God's kingdom.

I think what I'm *supposed* to believe about my longings is

Deep down, what I really believe about my longings is

If you have trouble identifying what you really believe, you can look at your decisions (page 50) and work backward to figure out the beliefs behind your decisions.

It's hard for me to trust God because

God deserves my trust because

*If God didn't hesitate to put everything on the line for us,
embracing our condition and exposing himself to the worst
by sending his own Son, is there anything else he wouldn't
gladly and freely do for us? And who would dare tangle
with God by messing with one of God's chosen? Who
would dare even point a finger? The One who died for us—
who was raised to life for us!—is in the presence of God at
this very moment sticking up for us.*
Romans 8:31-34, MSG

DECISIONS

Based on our beliefs, we make decisions.

First, we decide on the *ruling passion* that will be the driving force behind what we say and do. This ruling passion is a filter through which we see everything, gauge priorities, judge other people, and allot time and money. The word *passion* is derived from old French and Latin roots that mean "suffering, pain, or some disorder of body or spirit." It's also defined as "any kind of feeling by which the mind is powerfully affected or moved."

Second, we decide on the *actions* we will take to live out that ruling passion. Ruling passions can be holy or foolish:

THE PASSION TO MATTER
I want to be the most beautiful, or the most talented, or the smartest.
I want enough money to make people treat me as important.
I want to be loved unconditionally.
I want to do something worthwhile.

THE PASSION FOR SECURITY
I want the security of a marriage, no matter what.
I want to avoid pain.
I want to avoid change.
I want to feel safe amid trials.
I want to feel secure when things are changing.

THE PASSION FOR INTIMACY
I want to make someone love me.
I want to feel heard by and connected to someone.
I want to be sexually fulfilled.
I want to feel connected or fulfilled, *no matter what.*

THE PASSION FOR SUCCESS
>I want to be all I can be.
>>I want to avoid failure.
>>>I want to transcend failure.
>>>>I want to make a lot of money to prove I'm a success.
>>>>>I want everyone to like me.

THE PASSION FOR SPIRITUALITY
>I want abundant life.
>>I want a God who makes me feel good all the time.
>>I want an exciting spiritual life.
>I want a spiritual practice that makes me feel calm and in control.
>>I want to know the real God, whatever it costs.
>>>I want to live out my reason for being.

More than anything else, I want

I feel like I'll die without

Decisions

For me, the most important thing in life is

44

I spend a lot of money on

I give a lot of time to

I've made huge sacrifices to get

Some of the sacrifices I've made are

God's bounty is limited only by us,
not by His resources, power, or
willingness to give. . . . God always
intervenes when you put His agenda
before yours and go for it!
—*Bruce Wilkinson*

I'm confused about my ruling passion because

The ruling passion that drives me is

Things I have done because of my ruling passion are

The foolish aspects of my ruling passion are

The wise aspects of my ruling passion are

The passions I would like to rule my life are

To be ruled by those passions, I would have to believe

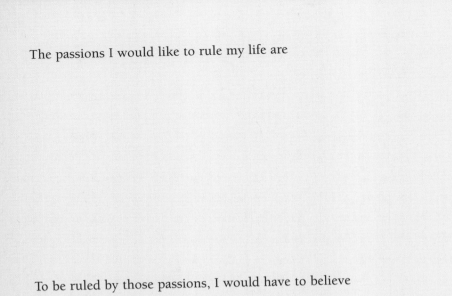

The hard part for me in believing

What helps me believe

I choose to believe

A decision I am making about my ruling passion

A decision I am making about my actions

The help I need in following through

People who will support my beliefs and decisions

When I think about my past and present decisions, I feel

What I'd like to say to God about my past and present decisions is

In this process of changing my ruling passion and decisions, something good I can do to nurture myself is

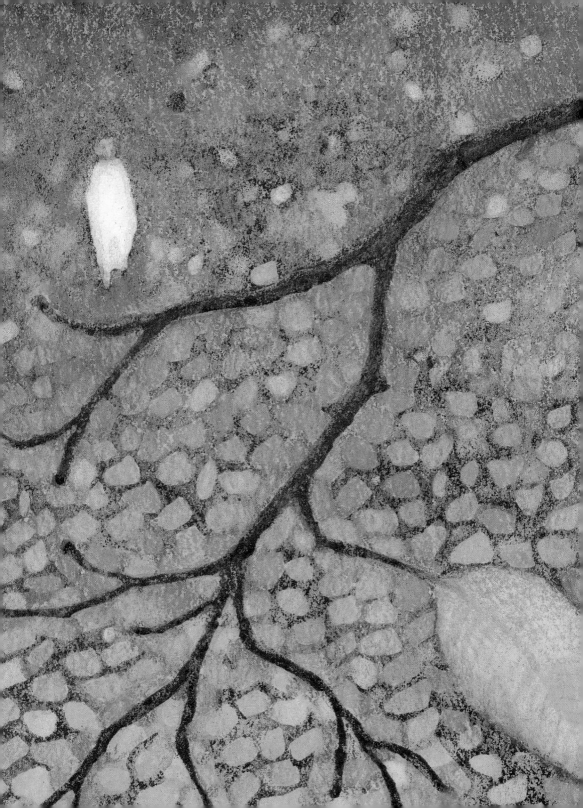

My Fears

Some fears are smart:

   🙠 God is an all-powerful, consuming fire that will consume anyone who approaches Him with arrogance or contempt.

   🙠 Death is going to happen to you. Plan ahead.

   🙠 Skipping exams at school and forgetting to file a tax return are two bad ideas.

   🙠 If you let your five-year-old wander around in a city unattended, something unpleasant will likely happen.

Smart fears motivate you to take responsibility for yourself and others. They are God-given instincts to run from danger, avert an accident, protect those you love, and bow in the presence of the One who alone deserves worship.

Smart fear shifts into slavish fear when it becomes obsessive and controlling. Usually the problem boils down to focusing and relying on self rather than God.

Smart fear bows before the Holy God and embraces His generous love. Slavish fear runs from Him, too obsessed with her unworthiness to focus on His offer of love.

Smart fear plans for death and takes reasonable precautions to avoid accidents and disease. Smart fear accepts God's solution to death. Slavish fear obsesses about death, accidents, or disease, or refuses to think about them at all. Slavish fear thinks it's up to self to protect her from death.

Smart fear studies for an exam and prays for help. Slavish fear stays up all night worrying about an exam and can't trust God's help.

Smart fear cares for her child and entrusts the child to God. Slavish fear tries to control the child's every experience.

Typically, fear begins with a triggering event that makes us aware of danger or pain. We respond with a range of reactions and go on to some level of powerlessness and rage. At that point, we begin to negotiate inside ourselves. What will we do about the threat? This negotiation leads to a decision to resolve the situation constructively or destructively. The chain reaction looks like this:

FEARS: A CHAIN REACTION

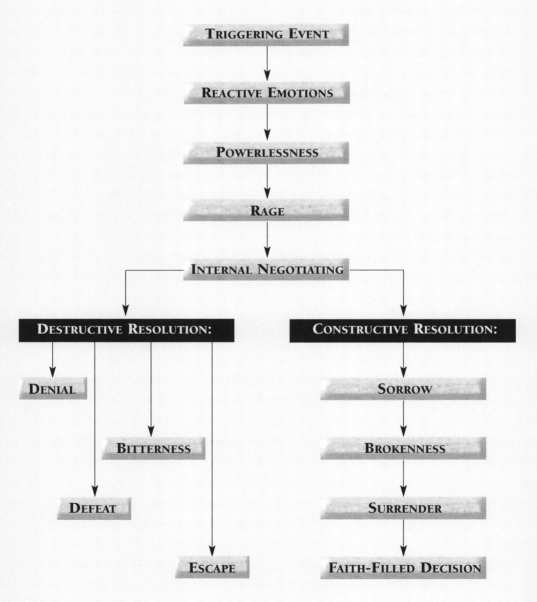

TRIGGERING EVENT

REACTIVE EMOTIONS

POWERLESSNESS

RAGE

INTERNAL NEGOTIATING

DESTRUCTIVE RESOLUTION:

DENIAL

BITTERNESS

DEFEAT

ESCAPE

CONSTRUCTIVE RESOLUTION:

SORROW

BROKENNESS

SURRENDER

FAITH-FILLED DECISION

TRIGGERS

A trigger launches your fear. It may be real or imagined, but it appears threatening, harmful, or painful.

What scares you?

THE FEAR OF THINGS THAT HAVEN'T HAPPENED—YET!
I'm afraid of heights—I might fall.
I'm afraid of crowds—I might suffocate.
I'm afraid of water—I might drown.
I'm afraid of getting sick.
I'm afraid of losing my job.
I'm afraid of not getting into college.
I'm afraid my husband will have an accident.
I'm afraid of having another panic attack!

THE FEAR OF BEING VULNERABLE
I'm afraid of losing control.
I'm afraid of showing weakness.
I'm afraid of doing things less than perfectly.
I'm afraid of revealing my emotions.
I'm afraid of revealing my past.
I'm afraid people will laugh at me.
I'm afraid of being rejected.
I'm afraid of letting people know how fearful I am!

THE FEAR OF ABANDONMENT
I'm afraid of disappointing my parents.
I'm afraid of disappointing my boyfriend.
I'm afraid of disappointing people at church.
I'm afraid my husband will leave me.
I'm afraid no good man will ever stay with me.
I'm afraid another friend will betray me.
I'm afraid people will walk away if I fail.

THE FEAR OF TRUTH
I'm afraid to know what really happened.
I'm afraid to face what my family really was like.
I'm afraid to face the real state of my marriage.
I'm afraid to find out what my boyfriend does when I'm not there.
I'm afraid I'm losing my faith in God.

THE FEAR OF MAKING WRONG CHOICES
I'm afraid I'll be trapped in a bad relationship.
I'm afraid I'll lose the chance for a great career.
I'm afraid I'll be alone for the rest of my life.
I'm afraid I'll never have a baby.
I'm afraid I'll fail if I try.
I'm afraid I won't be able to handle success.

I'm afraid

I'm afraid

I'm afraid

I'm afraid

I'm afraid

I run away when

I shut down when

I fight back when

I panic when

I explode when

I feel shy when

I can't be myself around

I don't know what I'm afraid of

I think I get scared because

I can't be myself because

I don't want to know the truth because

The fear of the Lord is the beginning of wisdom.
The fear of everything else is the end of wisdom.

I worry a lot

My big worries are

The worst thing that could happen would be

What I most want to avoid is

My little worries are

Worry works. If I worry hard enough,
what I'm worrying about never happens.

59

Is my fear a monster with huge jaws? A strangling snake? A dark thing? A blinding light? A smothering blanket?

Triggers

What if God were there, skewering the monster?

I wouldn't be afraid if

What I'd like to say to God about those triggering moments

Hold us in quiet through the age-long minute
While Thou art silent, and the wind is shrill:
Can the boat sink while Thou, dear Lord, art in it?
Can the heart faint that waiteth on Thy will?
—Amy Carmichael

61

REACTIONS

Your first honest reaction to a triggering event is almost involuntary:

Shock
Terror
Panic
Dread
Anxiety
Horror
Hurt
Anger

Shame
Outburst of rage
Wounded withdrawal
Pounding heart
Loss of breath
Numbness
Paralysis

In my chest, fear feels like

In my head, fear feels like

In my body, fear feels like

When I'm threatened

I can't sleep

When I can't sleep, my body feels

What keeps me awake is

When I can't sleep, I

63

POWERLESSNESS

Unless your initial reaction demolishes the danger, you probably feel some level of powerlessness. You're apparently alone and unprotected before a scary, powerful person or situation. You're not in control the way you'd like to be. You might think:

There's nothing I can do to change this situation!

There's nothing I can do to stop this panic reaction!

I can't handle this!

I'm not good enough!

I'm not strong enough!

I'm burning out!

I'm all alone!

What makes me feel helpless

When I feel helpless, I

The truth about my helplessness is

Psalm 18

I love you, O LORD, my strength.
The LORD is my rock, my fortress and my deliverer;
my God is my rock, in whom I take refuge. . . .
The cords of death entangled me;
the torrents of destruction overwhelmed me.
The cords of the grave coiled around me;
the snares of death confronted me.
In my distress I called to the LORD;
I cried to my God for help.
From his temple he heard my voice;
my cry came before him, into his ears. . . .
He reached down from on high and took hold of me;
he drew me out of deep waters.
He rescued me from my powerful enemy,
from my foes, who were too strong for me.
They confronted me in the day of my disaster,
but the LORD was my support.
He brought me out into a spacious place;
he rescued me because he delighted in me. . . .
You, O LORD, keep my lamp burning;
my God turns my darkness into light.
With your help I can advance against a troop;
with my God I can scale a wall. . . .
He makes my feet like the feet of a deer;
he enables me to stand on the heights. . . .
You broaden the path beneath me,
so that my ankles do not turn.

RAGE

If we were sinless, we'd instantly shift our focus from our helplessness to God's sufficiency. But the natural human reaction is to try to regain control. Rage is the usual fuel for the control response. Rage may feel like hot anger or cold determination. We may not literally shake our fists at God or the world, but that's what rage boils down to. Underneath whatever actual words go through our heads and out our mouths are buried thoughts like these:

> *"I hate what is happening here, and I won't have it! I refuse to feel helpless and dependent! God, You have let me down by allowing me to experience this situation or emotion, and I can't trust You anymore. I'm determined to find a better way to resolve my feelings."*

For me, rage looks like

When I feel out of control, I

What I want to say to God or the world about this is

When I get mad, I want to

If I didn't feel silly acting like a two-year-old, I would

What I really want God to do to the person who hurt me is

Rage

May those who seek my life
  be disgraced and put to shame;
may those who plot my ruin
  be turned back in dismay.
May they be like chaff before the wind,
  with the angel of the LORD driving
    them away;
may their path be dark and slippery,
  with the angel of the LORD pursuing
    them.
                    —Psalm 35:4-6

Sometimes you have a good reason to be angry. It's okay to express your anger to God. He wants to hear it.

I feel betrayed.

Here's what happened:

Betray. The word is an eighth of an inch above "betroth" in the dictionary, but a world from "betroth" in life. It's a weapon found only in the hands of one you love. . . . Betrayal is mutiny. It's a violation of a trust, an inside job.
—Max Lucado

What I want to do about this betrayal is

Rage

Instead, I'm going to

> *This isn't the neighborhood bully*
> *mocking me—I could take that. . . .*
> *It's you! We grew up together!*
> *You! My best friend!*
> *Those long hours of leisure as we walked*
> *arm in arm, God a third party to our conversation.*
> *—Psalm 55:12-14,* MSG

Forgiving someone doesn't mean saying what she did was okay. It doesn't require you to let her do it again. Rather, forgiveness involves:

- Canceling the debt; mentally tearing up the note that says, "she owes me"

- Letting go of the desire to make her pay for what she's done

- Being open to the possibility of a restored relationship to the extent that the other person's behavior makes that possible

- Longing for her to become fully the person God made her to be so that a restored relationship will be possible

- Wanting good for her

- Doing good to her even if she doesn't repent

It's possible to do good to someone and to want God's best for him even while insisting, "No, I will not be alone with you because you are not a safe person. No, I will not pretend like nothing happened." Wise boundaries are not the same as holding a grudge and punishing someone.

Also, forgiveness is not always a once-for-all event—you decide to release your anger, and it never comes back. Often, forgiveness is a process and a repeated choice. Jesus told Peter he might have to forgive someone 70x7 times (Matthew 18:22).

"If you see your friend going wrong, correct him. If he responds, forgive him. Even if it's personal against you and repeated seven times through the day, and seven times he says, 'I'm sorry, I won't do it again,' forgive him."
—*Luke 17:3-4,* MSG

71

If I decide not to make him/her pay,

What keeps me from forgiving is

I don't want to have a restored relationship because

Rage

A restored relationship would look like

What would I need to see in his/her life in order to have a restored relationship?

Even if I don't fully *trust* him/her, I can *care* and *do good to* him/her by

If I forgive

If I don't forgive

My prayer for this person is

Rage

74

Depression is often anger turned inward toward yourself. Maybe you don't feel you have a right to be angry. Maybe you're afraid you'll be punished if you express anger. Maybe you blame yourself rather than others.

Depression cuts you off from God and other people who would like to love you. Instead of being ashamed of it, you can use it as a clue that something in your life needs to be addressed.

When depression goes beyond the mild level of "feeling the blues," it can indicate that certain chemicals in your brain may be too low. If you feel blue for a long period or if your depression is intense, it's a good idea to talk to a doctor about it. Don't tell yourself, "Depression is a sin and I should be able to shake it off without help." Even if there's sin involved (and there may not be), where did you get the idea that you should be able to shake sin off without help?

Depression feels like

I'm depressed because

I feel angry at myself because

I don't feel angry at anyone else because

I wish

Rage

I think my depression is telling me

NEGOTIATION

The trigger, reaction, powerlessness, and rage can all happen quickly and almost involuntarily. At this point, you have a chance to decide what to do. You'll start negotiating inside yourself: Should I rely on myself to fix this situation? If so, what will I do? Should I give up and wallow in defeat? Should I throw all my trust on God to resolve the situation? What would that look like? What are the pros and cons?

You can choose:

Denial		Sorrow
Defeat	or	Brokenness
Bitterness		Surrender
Escape		Faith

Your decision will reflect your deepest beliefs about God, yourself, and life.

Right now, the situation that is bothering me the most is

If I rely on myself, the worst thing that could happen is

If I rely on God, the worst thing that could happen is

If I give up and accept defeat, the worst thing would be

The advantages of relying on myself are

The advantages of relying on God are

I don't trust God because

I don't trust myself because

I don't trust others because

I don't trust anyone right now.

That's because

In order to start trusting again, I need to

I am most inclined to trust _____ because

DENIAL

If you decide not to rely on God, you'll spiral into a cycle of denial, defeat, bitterness, and escape.

Maybe you know your fear or anger reflects sin and a lack of faith. You can try to pretend it isn't there. Ironically, we often get angry because a situation leaves us feeling out of control. Then our emotions feel out of control and we get angry that we're angry! We try harder to control our anger just as we try to control everything else.

Maybe the situation simply scares you so much that you don't want to face it. You'd rather pretend it's not there or doesn't bother you.

I don't want to deal with

because

Denial

When I kept it all inside,
my bones turned to powder,
my words became daylong groans.
Psalm 32:3, MSG

To protect myself from feeling fear, I

To avoid feeling anger, I

To keep people from knowing I feel _____, I

On the outside I appear

On the inside I'm

I don't want to admit

because

If I admitted

Denial

then

Burying anger or fear doesn't help to resolve the issues, and it doesn't honor God. He knows what's in your heart. He longs for you to acknowledge your feelings and allow Him to carry you beyond them. Something concrete you can do to acknowledge your feelings is to write a letter to God.

Dear God,

DEFEAT

I'm the helpless victim of circumstances.

What makes me think this is

There's nothing I can do about this situation because

There's nothing I can do about my emotions because

God won't help because

84

How I act defeated

What other people do when I act defeated

Acting like a helpless victim gets me

Seeing myself as a helpless victim protects me from

The trouble with giving up is

85

BITTERNESS

My problems are not my fault!

The ones who are responsible are

because

God could have

The benefits of blaming others

Bitterness

The drawbacks of blaming others

Instead of blaming others, I could

Why shouldn't I blame God?

ESCAPE

Right about now, a desert island is looking good.

My favorite escape route is

      Eating ice cream
              Drinking alcohol
                     Taking pills
                           Watching TV
    Working late
           Working out
                 Trying to look perfect
                        Volunteering at church
                      Reading

The drawbacks of escaping are

Make fun of your inner monsters. They hate it! Draw your four friends/ enemies: Denial, Defeat, Bitterness, and Escape. You can cut out pictures from magazines or comics too. If you'd rather use words, write about why the Fab Four are completely ridiculous.

RENEGOTIATION

Self-reliance isn't working out for me.

In order to rely on God, I'll need

What do I think about relying on God?

Courage is fear that has said its prayers.
—C. S. Lewis

For me, the unknown is

Maybe if I learn more about the unknown, I won't be so scared. Here's what I can do.

Renegotiation

SORROW

The shift from anger, depression, bitterness, and defeat comes when we stop trying to "fix" our feelings or situation and begin to grieve honestly and deeply. We live in a "groaning" creation where imperfect people hurt and disappoint us. That's sad. When powerful people abuse their positions and make us fearful, that's sad. When we are abandoned by someone we expected to love us, that's sad. Yet when we let the sorrow of a sinful world penetrate us, something else happens. When we cease playing the blame game and let ourselves grieve, we change.

I'm sad.

I feel like an open wound.

Here's what happened.

Lamentations 3

I am one who has seen affliction
       under the rod of God's wrath. . . .
My soul is bereft of peace;
       I have forgotten what happiness is;
so I say, "Gone is my glory,
       and all that I had hoped for from the LORD."

The thought of my affliction and my homelessness
       is wormwood and gall!
My soul continually thinks of it
       and is bowed down within me.
But this I call to mind,
       and therefore I have hope:

The steadfast love of the LORD never ceases,
       his mercies never come to an end;
they are new every morning;
       great is your faithfulness.
"The Lord is my portion," says my soul,
       "therefore I will hope in him."

The LORD is good to those who wait for him,
       to the soul that seeks him.
It is good that one should wait quietly
       for the salvation of the LORD. . . .
For the LORD will not
       reject forever.
Although he causes grief, he will have compassion
       according to the abundance of his steadfast love;
for he does not willingly afflict
       or grieve anyone. (NRSV)

93

I feel rejected.

The worst rejection I ever felt was

When I feel rejected I usually

What I need God to do

Sorrow

What I'm going to do this time is

94

There are so many things to feel sad about.

Sorrow

Restore our fortunes, O LORD,
like streams in the Negev.
Those who sow in tears
will reap with songs of joy.
He who goes out weeping,
carrying seed to sow,
will return with songs of joy,
carrying sheaves with him.
Psalm 126:4-6

Feeling sad scares me.

I don't know what to do.

I need help!

I will call

Sorrow

I will ask God

Strangely, it feels good to let myself feel sad.

In my sadness, I think God wants to tell me

*"You're blessed when you feel you've lost
what is most dear to you.
Only then can you be embraced
by the One most dear to you."*
Matthew 5:4, MSG

BROKENNESS

I've sinned.

I did what I shouldn't have done.

I didn't do what I should have done.

I learned God-worship
when my pride was shattered.
Heart-shattered lives ready for love
don't for a moment escape God's notice.
Psalm 51:17, MSG

I've avoided admitting my sin because

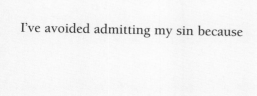

What I want to say to God about my sin is

I think what God wants to say to me is

God, make a fresh start in me,
shape a Genesis week
from the chaos of my life.
Psalm 51:10, MSG

I've also been carrying around a lot of false guilt.

These feelings weren't sinful.

These longings weren't sinful.

Brokenness

One of the primary names for the Holy Spirit is "the Comforter." And one of the primary names for the devil, who likes to impersonate the Holy Spirit, is "the Accuser."
—Jim Cymbala

I'm not powerful enough to fix this situation.

Brokenness

But God

I need

We carry this precious Message
around in the unadorned clay pots of
our ordinary lives. That's to prevent
anyone from confusing God's
incomparable power with us.
2 Corinthians 4:7, MSG

101

I need help.

I can ask (friends? counseling service? minister? mentor? professional association?
family? help lines? small groups? God?)

What's the worst thing that could happen if I tell someone?

Brokenness

What's the best thing?

SURRENDER

Okay! I'm laying down my guns and coming out with my hands up. I can't change it, so I accept it.

I have to let go of

The difference between surrender to God and defeat is

I'm surrendering my fears

I'm surrendering my anger

I'm surrendering my plan to stay in control

I'm surrendering my frustration that I'm not perfect

I'm surrendering

I'm surrendering

I'm surrendering   *Surrender*

I'm surrendering

I'm surrendering

The scary part of surrendering

The good part of surrendering

I feel 100 pounds lighter.

The discipline of confession brings an end to pretense. . . . Honesty leads to confession, and confession leads to change.
—*Richard Foster*

FAITH-FILLED DECISION

Once we surrender the situation, the person, and our feelings—placing them all in God's hands—we can make choices that reflect trust in God. A faith-filled decision might be:

> Facing the truth about what happened
>> Revealing who we are to others
>>> Taking a risk when before we would have held back
> Waiting trustfully when before we would have frantically
>> taken action to be in control
>>> Doing what's right and accepting the consequences

A faith-filled decision isn't a blind step into the darkness. We don't have faith in faith, nor in ourselves—we have faith in the God who made us, protects us, intends good for us, and has a vital purpose for us to fulfill in the world.

What I need to do is

What scares me most is

From God I need

From others I need

Nothing can happen to me that will ultimately destroy me. I am safe with God.

Therefore

Dumb things I've done to feel safer

Good things that can help me feel safe

I'll start today by

Faith-filled Decision

If I really trust God, then I'll

Faith-filled Decision

In order to get from here to there, I need to

I'll begin by

My biggest fear right now

What I think God wants to say to that fear

Faith-filled Decision

What I'm going to do

My Gifts

One of the best things about dealing with our fears and longings is becoming free to give and receive love. Maybe you've admired those people who have significant positive influence in others' lives, but you've thought, "Me? I could never make a difference for someone else. I'm just barely able to take care of myself." But the more you surrender your longings and fears to God, and the more you move into faith-filled decisions, the more you'll have inside you to give away.

What would happen if you decided to influence lives on purpose? Not in a bossy, busybody way, but in a way that pays attention to what God is already doing in people? Here are seven simple things Jesus did that transformed the people He encountered:

> He cultivated His own prayer life, so His ears and eyes were constantly open to what His Father was saying and doing.

> He spent time with people, and as opportunities for significant conversation arose, He seized them.

> He told stories that helped people grasp important truths.

> He asked great questions.

> He acted with hands-on compassion when people had needs.

> He loved unconditionally.

> He cast a vision for what people could be and do.

You probably have strengths in at least a few of these areas. You probably can grow in the others. God has designed you with your own unique style of loving influence. Why not explore it?

When I think about influencing others' lives

I dream of having this effect on the people in my world

In order to do this, I'd need

PRAYER

"Jesus often withdrew to lonely places and prayed" (Luke 5:16). This was the secret to the rest of His life, the hours and hours He spent working among the poor and sick, training stubborn disciples, and standing up to vicious critics. Jesus' life was full of unmet longings and scary situations, yet He consistently made faith-filled decisions because He was grounded in prayer.

My ideal prayer life

My actual prayer life these days

My biggest barriers to prayer

What I'll need to do to overcome them

I will begin by

My best times for prayer are

My favorite place to pray is

"Our Father in heaven,
Reveal who you are.
Set the world right;
Do what's best—
as above, so below.
Keep us alive with three square meals.
Keep us forgiven with you
and forgiving others.
Keep us safe
from ourselves and the Devil.
You're in charge!
You can do anything you want!
You're ablaze in beauty!
Yes. Yes. Yes."
—Matthew 6:9-13, MSG

Dear God,

I need to talk to you about prayer

I asked God for

This is what happened

What I think about that is

119

Thank you, God, for

Thank you for

Thank you for

Thank you for

Thank you for

Thank you for

Thank you for

Thank you for

Thank you for

Prayer

120

RELATIONSHIPS

Being a positive influence in others' lives doesn't require you to pack your schedule with extra tasks. Chances are that you already encounter people in the course of any given week to whom you could offer God's love.

I have a friend

What I pray for her

Something from my prayer life that might encourage her

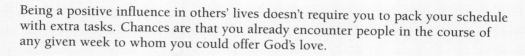

I could pray with my friend

When?

Where?

She is a friend. She gathers the pieces and gives them back to me in all the right order.
— Toni Morrison

People in my life who already know God but need more of Him

People in my life who don't know Him

To build these relationships, I am already

I could

Treating people with Jesus' kind of love means

I'm already

I could grow in

Relationships

I will begin by

I'm really busy.

What busyness does to my relationships

I'm too busy to have new relationships. But here are some things I can do with people even though I don't have a lot of extra time.

In the midst of busyness, I can show someone love today.

God is at work in my life.

If I let someone in on my real life, they'd think

What they might learn about God

Relationships

If I could tell a friend one thing about God's love today, it would be

I could say this without words by

Relationships

STORIES

Stories can teach complex theological truths in ways that don't intimidate or threaten. Someone may doubt your spiritual beliefs, but she might be receptive to a story of your actual experience with life or God.

Stories connect storyteller to story hearer with companionship and comfort. They intrigue their hearers, keeping them guessing about the outcomes. You could push someone away if you lecture her on how she should run her life, but you could draw her closer by telling a story of how you solved a problem in your own life.

A story I could tell about my family

Where is God in my story?

A story I could tell about my longings

"You've been given insight into
God's kingdom — you know how it
works. But to those who can't see it
yet, everything comes in stories,
creating readiness, nudging them
toward receptive insight."
Mark 4:11, MSG

129

A story I could tell about overcoming one of my fears

Someone who might benefit from my story

How my story is relevant to her

Stories

The scary part of telling my story

How I'm going to deal with my fear

I'll begin by

My friend needs a chance to tell her story.

When can I make time to listen to her?

How can I help her feel comfortable?

QUESTIONS

Sometimes the most helpful thing you can do for someone is to ask her questions. Instead of giving advice, you can ask questions that help her think through her own decision. If she's hurting, questions help her put words to her pain so she doesn't have to carry it alone. Questions show that you're genuinely interested in her.

A good question:
- Requires more than a yes-or-no answer
- Doesn't put words into her mouth
- Doesn't subtly accuse her
- Invites thoughts or feelings or stories

Here are some good questions:
- What were your growing-up years like?
- What's your best memory of your father? Your mother?
- What is your favorite old movie?
- What kind of music do you like?
- In what part of your life do you feel vulnerable?
- What keeps you from being as close to the Lord as you'd like to be?
- If you had a completely free day, what would you do?
- What are your hobbies? What are your passions?
- If money were not an issue, what would you do with the rest of your life?
- What's the biggest roadblock between you and your dream?
- In what two specific areas would you like to see yourself grow during the next one to three years?
- What's the biggest answer to prayer you've ever experienced?
- What do you like best about your job? Least?
- How can I help you?
- How can I pray for you?

I know somebody who needs to talk.

Some good questions for her would be

If I ask personal questions, she might

I asked some questions

Here's what happened

When I'm struggling to deal
with a tough situation, she
points me in the right
direction by asking, "What
does the Scripture say about
this?" and "How may I pray
for you?" Those two key
questions . . . immediately shift
the focus back to where it
belongs: on our Father in
Heaven.
—Leola Floren

PRACTICAL COMPASSION

Sometimes talking and listening are all someone needs. Sometimes she needs more. Compassion involves:

> Seeing someone's need or suffering
> Feeling sad about the need; suffering with the person
> Taking action to address the need

I've experienced compassion from others.

Here's what I needed

Here's what happened

Needs I've noticed

Sometimes I wish I didn't notice people's needs! It makes me feel

When I see someone suffering, I

I think that's because

What I'd like to do is

Practical Compassion

What have you done
today that only a
Christian would have done?
—Corrie ten Boom

I get overwhelmed.

Practical Compassion

I could avoid compassion fatigue if I

I'll begin by

Some practical things I could do

    Cook a meal or pick up take-out food
      Offer to baby-sit
        Remember her with a card or call on sad anniversaries
       Do laundry or clean house
       Take her a treat

Practical Compassion

Someone who just needs a touch or a hug

Someone who needs me to cry with her

UNCONDITIONAL LOVE

People need to know you'll still love them if they get sick, get older, gain weight, get bad grades, or make a dumb choice. Unconditional love doesn't give someone blanket permission to be cruel to you or others without consequences. It does give her blanket permission to mess up and try again. Love moves through a process:

- *Kindness*: I'm with you. I'm for you, not against you.
- *Encouragement*: You're on the right track. You can handle it. I'll help.
- *Challenge*: We both know what you need to do. You can do it. Let's get going.

I know someone who needs to be loved unconditionally.

Here's her situation

Here's how I can be kind

Encouraging

Unconditional Love

Challenging

I have some questions about unconditional love.

Unconditional Love

> Love never gives up.
> Love cares more for others than for self.
> Love doesn't want what it doesn't have.
> Love doesn't strut,
> Doesn't have a swelled head,
> Doesn't force itself on others,
> Isn't always "me first,"
> Doesn't fly off the handle,
> Doesn't keep score of the sins of others,
> Doesn't revel when others grovel,
> Takes pleasure in the flowering of truth,
> Puts up with anything,
> Trusts God always,
> Always looks for the best,
> Never looks back,
> But keeps going to the end.
> —1 Corinthians 13:4-7, MSG

I've loved someone and gotten burned.

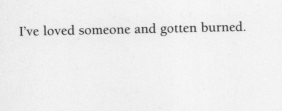

What I've learned about love

Unconditional Love

What I'll do differently

On Betrayal and Forgiveness,
see pages 66–74

I need help to love well.

What's the worst thing that could happen if I risk it?

What's the best thing that could happen if I risk it?

Someone has loved me unconditionally.

It made a difference

Now I want to

Unconditional Love

VISION

When was the last time someone told you what you uniquely contribute to the world? Can't remember? The people you know probably can't remember either. You could be the one to tell them!

Casting vision for another person doesn't mean telling her what she should do with her life. It's not bossy. It includes:

- Noticing what she's doing
- Letting her know you think she's valuable
- Affirming the strengths and gifts you've seen her show
- Sharing your sense of your own mission in life
- Telling her something specific you've seen her contribute
- Freeing her to do something she's good at, and not do things she's not good at
- Giving her a task to try
- Giving her enough training that she feels prepared
- Giving her enough freedom to accomplish her mission in her own way
- Giving her time to grow into her potential

It's especially valuable to cast vision for someone who is younger than you in age or spiritual maturity.

I know someone with potential. Her name is

I've seen her do

I think her strengths/gifts/godly qualities are

I could help her move forward with God's vision for her by

Vision

There is no magic in
small plans. When I
consider my ministry,
I think of the world.
Anything less
than that would not be
worthy of Christ nor
His will for my life.
—Henrietta Mears

If I could do something out of love for God, here's what I'd do.

To turn my dream into reality I need to

A year from today it will be

By that time I think God wants me to be

To live out my purpose and calling, I will need to take some steps.

Do you have a reason for being, a focused sense of purpose in your life?. . . Do you want to go beyond success to significance? Have you come to realize that self-reliance always falls short and that world-denying solutions provide no answer in the end? Listen to Jesus of Nazareth; answer His call.
—Os Guinness

For information on scheduling Carol Kent or Karen Lee-Thorp as a speaker for your group, please contact Speak Up Speaker Services. You may call us toll free at (888) 870-7719, e-mail Speakupinc@aol.com, or visit our website at www.SpeakUpSpeakerServices.com.

Afterthoughts

Afterthoughts

153

Afterthoughts

Afterthoughts

155

Afterthoughts

Afterthoughts

Afterthought

Afterthoughts

160